Light & Life

AN INDUCTIVE BIBLE STUDY
ON PSALM 119

By
Erin H. Warren

feasting on truth

Copyright © 2021, 2023 by Erin H. Warren
Published by Headley Warren Productions LLC
Orlando, Florida
www.FeastingOnTruth.com

ISBN 978-1-959305-07-1

For Tammy
Your passion for the Word fueled mine, and your love of Psalm 119 inspired me to write this study. Thank you for showing me the deliberateness of God, the power of His Word, and the joy of walking through the wilderness with our Beloved.

contents

contents

start here

I was sitting in a circle of women in my living room. This wasn't our first Bible study together; it was probably our third or fourth go-around. As we shared our prayer requests, I was struck by something. Some of our prayer requests were the same as they had been a year before. Struggles and fears still gripped us. It was the first time I wondered: *Why haven't we made progress? Why aren't we overcoming?*

I had heard verses that talked about overcoming sin. I knew the goal of my Christian life was to become more like Jesus. I knew we were called to not look like the world and instead be filled with the fruit of the Spirit. But something was missing.

Years later, I was sitting in my seat at a women's conference, expectant and ready to hear from God. The speaker was Jen Wilkin, whom I had only recently heard of, and this quote from her forever changed my perspective on studying the Word of God:

> *We cannot be content being curators of other people's opinions about a book we cannot be bothered to read ourselves.* — Jen Wilkin

That was it. That was the light-bulb moment when I realized what was missing: personal study of God's Word. I had merely been a librarian, curating other people's study findings and revelations. I had never learned to study God's Word for myself. There are a myriad of reasons why we don't study His Word firsthand: too busy, not equipped with the right tools, misinformation about women and the Bible. I could go on and on, but I think if we truly knew the power the Word of God has in our lives, we wouldn't be able to put it down. It is the very source of life, and a light to guide us as we navigate that life here on earth. This is why I chose Psalm 119. This passage gives us the most comprehensive look at the power and benefits provided to us in the Word of God. This is not power that can be mustered up in our own human strength or learned from reading any other book. It's a power that can only come from the One who created the universe. In his book, *The Golden Alphabet*, Charles Spurgeon writes this:

7

The best compositions of men are soon depleted, for they are cisterns and not springing fountains. You enjoy them very much when you first come across them, and you think you could hear them a hundred times over; but you cannot actually do so, for you soon find them wearisome. A man very quickly eats too much honey, and even children are sickened by sweets eventually. In the same way, all human books grow stale after a time, but with the Word of God, the desire to study it increases, while the more you know of it, the less you think you know.[1]

It's not a bad thing to read other books and do fill-in-the-blank studies, but they will not do for you what God's Word can do for you. Only God's Word will stand the test of time. Only God's Word is a well of living water that continually brings refreshment. Now, the more I study the Bible, the more I *want* to study the Bible. Studying Scripture firsthand changed me. I found I was memorizing Scripture, remembering His character, and overcoming in ways I never had before. And can I let you in on a little secret? It was *way* easier than I ever expected.

My passion is to encourage and equip women to discover God's truths for themselves and provide the resources and space to do so. I'm so glad you are here! Studying this way changed my life, and it can change yours too.

This type of study is called inductive Bible study. That can be an intimidating word. It simply means studying with your own heart and mind first, trusting the Holy Spirit to do what He promises to do (John 14:26) before turning to other sources. It's learning to ask the right questions of Scripture and read through a God-centered lens versus a me-centered lens (more on this in a moment).

I designed this study to help you pull out the details, see the character of God, and ask the right questions of this passage. It's not your typical study book. I won't lead you, but instead walk alongside you and guide you as you discover the truths in Psalm 119 for yourself.

A LITTLE BACKGROUND INFORMATION

Context is one of the most important steps of Bible study and one we often skip (or rely on someone else to tell us). Answering a few questions before we start helps us better interpret what we are reading. You can find a set of questions I typically ask before starting any Bible study on page 20.

Because Psalm 119 is a chapter (not a book), many study Bibles don't include extensive context information. You may have to do a little more digging to find the answers. But let me help you out a little. Psalm 119 is an acrostic poem with twenty-two stanzas, each stanza consists of eight verses and begins with a successive letter of the Hebrew alphabet. We miss this last detail in English, so most Bibles will put the name of the Hebrew letter at the beginning of each section.

These 176 verses all have one common thread: the Word. Almost every single verse uses a synonym for Scripture. On the surface, it may seem repetitive, but I encourage you to dig deep. When you do, you will see how each verse is different. Pay attention to the slight nuances in the author's words. Oh, and on that note, we don't know who wrote this psalm. But many scholars believe it was David.

---

1   *The Golden Alphabet: An Exposition of Psalm 119*, Charles Spurgeon, Aneko Press, Revised Edition Copyright 2018, page xi

THE PLAN

I broke this book into twenty-two sections, one for each stanza. For each one, you will write out the passage. I'm a big believer in writing Scripture—it draws our attention to each word, and we notice details we sometimes skip as we read. Because of that, there is space to write the eight verses for each section. When you are done, you will have written out the longest psalm! Plus, it's only eight verses at a time. You can do it!

Next, there are a few questions to answer: the synonyms used for the Word, the characteristics of the Word, and the benefits of the Word. I teach Bible study from a God-centered view (see page 11 for more on this). To fully understand our position, we must first know God. God's Word is His character. In this study, we will be pulling out the characteristics of God and His Word. Example: "But you are near, O LORD, and all your commandments are true" (Psalm 119:151). In this verse, the author points us to God's omnipresence ("You are near"), but also His Word is true. Because God is true, His Word is also true. (For lists of names and characteristics of God, see pages 12–13.)

Psalm 119:130 says, "The unfolding of your words gives light; it imparts understanding to the simple." The Hebrew word for *unfolding* means "opening" or "entrance." Think of His Word as a doorway. When we open His Word, it's like opening a door. The light spills out, and we enter into His glorious presence. There, He gives us understanding, no matter how "simple" we are. As you study each stanza and make lists of the characteristics and benefits of the Word, pray. Ask God to open the door and give light and understanding as you study. This is a promise, and He is faithful to keep His promises. I've also given you space to record your own revelations. And if you want more guidance on how to study, I've outlined the four simple questions I use to study on pages 207–210.

I want this to be doable for you, so I've kept it simple. (Remember when I said studying this way is easier than I thought?!) Each week, we will study three stanzas (except for Week 1). At the end of each week, you will find space for teaching notes and group notes. You'll also find a page to go deeper with additional Scripture about God's Word. Companion teachings are available on Season 4 of the Feasting on Truth podcast and on YouTube at youtube.com/c/erinhwarren. Links are also available on FeastingOnTruth.com/LightAndLife. You can also learn more about inductive Bible study in my book, *Feasting on Truth: Savor the Life-giving Word of God.*

Lastly, when studying a book of the Bible or long Scripture passage, I like to keep comprehensive lists to help me remember key themes and ideas. In the back of the book, in the Additional Notes section, there is a place to keep a complete list of the characteristics of the Word found throughout Psalm 119, as well as a place to list all of its benefits.

COMPANION TEACHINGS AND OTHER RESOURCES

I am committed to walking alongside you as you study Scripture inductively. I know you can do this, and I want to help you be successful. With the purchase of this book, I'm offering you access to what I'm calling *The Alongside Guide.* Scan the QR code or visit FeastingOnTruth.com/LightAndLife. There, you can sign up to access this valuable study bonus. You'll receive an email for each week of study  with helpful resources, including links to that week's teaching video and podcast, study notes with cross-references, quotes, characteristics of God, small group discussion questions, and more. It's everything you need to be successful in your study, and it gets delivered right to your inbox.

9

LET'S FEAST!

The word *feast* is rooted in abundance, and that's what awaits us in Scripture: a table laid out before us, not only for our essential nourishment, but also our enjoyment. Here are a few other tips to help you get started:

Move Slowly

Many Bible studies plow through Scripture, covering a chapter (or sometimes more) a day. There's certainly a time and place for that, but I've found when I move through Scripture slowly, (in this case, reading twenty-four verses a week), the Word of God soaks into my heart and mind deeply. I remember it more easily. I memorize it more effectively. What I love about this particular way of studying is that if I feel the need to stop and let a particular verse sink in, I can do so without feeling like I'm falling behind. It also leaves room for the Holy Spirit to do what only He can do. Which leads me to...

Let the Holy Spirit Guide You

Jesus gives us this promise in John 14:26: "But the Helper, the Holy Spirit, whom the Father will send in my name, he will teach you all things and bring to your remembrance all that I have said to you." Anytime I sit down to study, I start with prayer. I ask the Holy Spirit to teach me all the things and to help me remember all the things. That's His job. He's there to help, so invite Him into your time.

Don't Do This Alone

Personal time in the Word is so important, but equally important is that we also gather in community around the Word. Some of my deepest relationships are ones that were built on the discussion of Scripture. They are women who gathered around a table or in a living room or at a coffee shop, and we had hard conversations with the Word of Truth between us. Invite a few girlfriends to do this with you. I even included a fun recipe on page 213 you can make when you get together!

I recommend completing all of the homework on your own before listening to the teaching for the week. You can either listen on your own time or watch together with your group.

Finding time is hard. Women often tell me that they need to put their families first, that work is too crazy, or that they just don't have time to get together with other women for Bible study. Can I challenge you a bit? Is there any time more well spent than investing in our relationship with God? It's hard to pour out from an empty cup. We need to be constantly filled with Jesus, so we can pour out Jesus to our friends, family, and to God. Yes, this may look different in different seasons of life, but you won't regret making it a priority to spend time in the Word with other women.

I pray that through the words of Psalm 119, your passion for God's Word will be ignited, that you will crave His words more than any human's, and that you will grow in your confidence to open your Bible and study on your own.

I am cheering for you and praying for you! Happy feasting!

Because of Christ,

Erin H. Warren

10

knowing God

For too many years, I struggled with knowing how to interpret Scripture and apply these ancient words to my life. I did not know that God promises to equip us in studying Scripture through the Holy Spirit. And truthfully, I treated my Bible like one of those balls you shake, ask a question, flip over, and find your answer. Too many times I came to Scripture looking for an answer to my question, or I treated it like a yearbook—looking for all the pictures of myself.

Then, I began asking a different question, and my entire Bible study and life changed. I asked, "What does this say about God?" This shifted my perspective from a self-centered approach toward Scripture (where I am always asking, "What does this mean *to* me or *for* me?") to a God-centered approach—intentionally looking for and seeking out what each passage teaches me about God.

The Bible is not about me. It is first and foremost a book about God, and His name and character are written across every page. Our purpose on earth is to know God and make Him known, to love God and love others. But we can't love what we don't know; we can't worship what we don't know. And the primary way we know God is through His Word. The pursuit of knowledge about God is not optional; it's essential.

On the following pages, you will find two lists to help you: Names of God and Characteristics of God. It's not comprehensive, and there are spaces for you to add others as you discover more with each passage you read. Here are ways you can have a God-centered approach to your study:

- Ask, "What characteristics of God do I see in this passage?"

- Ask, "What names of God do I see in this passage?" (His names speak to His character.)

- Complete this sentence: Because God is _____, I can _____.

I understand there are different roles of the Trinity (God the Father, God the Son, God the Holy Spirit), but for the sake of simplicity (and especially as you are beginning), I think of them as One. If you need further help, visit www.FeastingOnTruth.com for more information and resources.

names of God

Abba Father

Adonai *(Lord, Master)*

Alpha and Omega

Bread of Life

Chief Cornerstone

Creator

Deliverer

El Elyon *(The Most High God)*

El Olam *(The Everlasting God)*

El Roi *(The God Who Sees Me)*

El Shaddai *(The Lord God Almighty)*

Elohim

Emmanuel

Everlasting Father

Great High Priest

Holy One

I AM

King of Kings

Lamb of God

Light of the World

Lion of Judah

Lord of Lords

Mighty God

Morning Star

Prince of Peace

Resurrection and the Life

Savior

Wonderful Counselor

Yahweh Amen *(The Lord is Truth)*

Yahweh Jireh *(The Lord Provides)*

Yahweh Nissi *(The Lord is my Banner)*

Yahweh-Raah *(The Lord is my Shepherd)*

Yahweh Rapha *(The Lord Heals)*

Yahweh Shalom *(The Lord is Peace)*

characteristics of God

Abounding in Steadfast Love

Compassionate

Deliberate

Faithful

Forgiving

Full of Grace

Good

Glorious

Gracious

Guide

Holy

Immutable *(Unchanging)*

Infinite

Invisible

Jealous

Just

Kind

Long-Suffering/Patient

Love

Merciful

Mighty

Omnipotent *(All-Powerful)*

Omnipresent

Omniscient *(All-Knowing)*

One

Perfect

Protector

Provider

Refuge/Help

Righteous

Self-Sufficient

Slow to Anger

Sovereign

Trustworthy

Truth

Wise

With Us

Light & Life

KNOWING GOD NOTES

small group guide

I am a firm believer in gathering together around the Word of God. It is at the heart of Feasting on Truth. As stated in *start here*, I believe that small group discussion is incredibly important when studying the Bible. I heard a pastor say, "Our time in the Word should be personal but never private." I do not believe we are called to study in isolation, and I believe it is in those places of isolation where Satan loves to tempt us. Discussing the passage in a small group setting (even if it's with only one other woman) helps confirm what the Holy Spirit taught you. It holds us accountable to truth. Not only that, but I learn so much from other women too. They will see truths within those passages that I miss. It helps build layers of understanding.

Leading a group is not nearly as difficult as it seems. I like to think of group leaders more like discussion leaders. A great discussion leader talks less than a third of the group time. You may need to speak first or jump in to get the conversation going, but the goal is to get the group talking.

Teaching for each chapter is available on Season 4 of the Feasting on Truth podcast or my YouTube channel: YouTube.com/c/erinhwarren.

Here are some other tips and a guide for your small group time:

Lead with authenticity
You do not have to have all the answers or have it all together to lead. I do not have it all together, and I fail miserably every day at doing what I know I should (Romans 7!). But I don't have to air all my dirty laundry to be authentic, and I never want my authenticity to enable sin in other people's lives. I've found that when I'm real about where I am and I invite women in to see how God is working on me in those areas, it invites them into authentic life change as well.

Set up a group text or use a group chat app
Connection throughout the week is key to building connection within your group. If you are not tech savvy or keeping up with a group chat isn't your strength, ask someone in the group to take charge of that. It's a great way to get others involved too! Throughout the week, you can check in on your group or share a verse or a particular insight into the passage.

Start with an ice breaker question
It doesn't have to be deep or spiritual, just something to get the conversation flowing. These types of questions are always a great way to help a group of women get to know each other.

15

Share your summary

Have the women share their summary for that week's passage. Depending on the size of your group, you may want to limit this to two to three women.

Ask: What characteristics of God did you see in this week's passage?

This works well "popcorn style." Let the women jump in with various names and characteristics of God and the verses that correspond. I usually add these to my own notes as well.

Use the weekly discussion questions

For this study, you can use the questions from the homework for discussion. For additional weekly discussion questions, go to FeastingOnTruth.com/LightAndLife and sign up to receive *The Alongside Guide* in your email. Each week, you'll get additional questions (as well as other resources and notes) delivered right to your inbox.

Share "Because God is" statements

This is a simple one, and I love it when everyone shares theirs! Depending on how long you have been together, some women in your group may not feel comfortable sharing the nitty-gritty of their lives. Having everyone share their "Because God is" statement is a way to engage the women who do not feel comfortable speaking up.

Share prayer requests

Sharing what is going on in our lives opens the door to build community and meet needs. I'll never forget sitting in a group when a woman shared that she needed prayer that she could pass her driving test. Across the table, another woman in the group spoke up and said, "I can help you learn to drive!" A couple months later, I received a picture of the two women holding a brand-new driver's license. It was incredible! Praying for one another is commanded, so allow time for this with your group. Pray with one another. Pray throughout the week. When we do this, we get to share an inheritance in what God is doing through the lives of others.

GROUP LIST

NAME	PHONE	EMAIL

Light & Life

WEEK 1

context

Light & Life

CONTEXT NOTES

See page 207 for more help on context.

Who wrote this psalm?

What do you know about this author?

To whom was it written?

When was it written?

What is the genre of this psalm?

What was the intent or purpose?

What was going on in history when this psalm was written?

20

CONTEXT NOTES

CONTEXT NOTES

Aleph

VERSES 1–8

ALEPH NOTES

PSALM 119:1-8

Write the stanza:

What are the synonyms for the Word used in this stanza?

Which characteristics of God and His Word are in this stanza?

What are the benefits of God's Word in this stanza?

How does the unfolding of this stanza give light (understanding) and life (sustain you)?

ALEPH NOTES

Write a prayer:

Because God's Word is:

    I can:

Light & Life

ALEPH NOTES

Light & Life

WEEK 1 TEACHING NOTES

Light & Life

WEEK 1 TEACHING NOTES

Light & Life

WEEK 1 GROUP NOTES

READ: 2 TIMOTHY 3:14–17

What truths does this passage reveal about God's Word?

Light & Life

WEEK 2

Beth

VERSES 9–16

Light & Life

BETH NOTES

PSALM 119:9-16

Write the stanza:

What are the synonyms for the Word used in this stanza?

Which characteristics of God and His Word are in this stanza?

What are the benefits of God's Word in this stanza?

How does the unfolding of this stanza give light (understanding) and life (sustain you)?

BETH NOTES

Write a prayer:

Because God's Word is:

    I can:

BETH NOTES

Gimel

VERSES 17–24

PSALM 119:17–24

Write the stanza:

Light & Life

What are the synonyms for the Word used in this stanza?

Which characteristics of God and His Word are in this stanza?

What are the benefits of God's Word in this stanza?

How does the unfolding of this stanza give light (understanding) and life (sustain you)?

GIMEL NOTES

Write a prayer: ....

....

....

....

....

....

....

....

....

....

....

....

....

....

....

....

....

....

....

....

....

....

Because God's Word is: ....

I can: ....

45

GIMEL NOTES

Daleth

VERSES 25-32

PSALM 119:25-32

Write the stanza:

Light & Life

DALETH NOTES

What are the synonyms for the Word used in this stanza?

Which characteristics of God and His Word are in this stanza?

What are the benefits of God's Word in this stanza?

How does the unfolding of this stanza give light (understanding) and life (sustain you)?

DALETH NOTES

Write a prayer:

Because God's Word is:

I can:

DALETH NOTES

Light & Life

WEEK 2 TEACHING NOTES

53

Light & Life

WEEK 2 TEACHING NOTES

Light & Life

WEEK 2 GROUP NOTES

Light & Life

GO DEEPER

READ: HEBREWS 4:12–13

What truths does this passage reveal about God's Word?

Light & Life

WEEK 3

He

VERSES 33-40

HE NOTES

PSALM 119:33-40

Write the stanza:

HE NOTES

What are the synonyms for the Word used in this stanza?

Which characteristics of God and His Word are in this stanza?

61

HE NOTES

What are the benefits of God's Word in this stanza?

How does the unfolding of this stanza give light (understanding) and life (sustain you)?

Light & Life

HE NOTES

Write a prayer: ....

....

....

....

....

....

....

....

....

....

....

....

....

....

....

....

....

....

....

....

....

....

....

Because God's Word is: ....

    I can: ....

THE NOTES

64

Waw

VERSES 41–48

Light & Life
WAW NOTES

PSALM 119:41–48

Write the stanza:

What are the synonyms for the Word used in this stanza?

Which characteristics of God and His Word are in this stanza?

What are the benefits of God's Word in this stanza?

How does the unfolding of this stanza give light (understanding) and life (sustain you)?

Light & Life

WAW NOTES

Write a prayer:

Because God's Word is:

I can:

Light & Life

WAW NOTES

Zayin

VERSES 49–56

PSALM 119:49-56

Write the stanza:

What are the synonyms for the Word used in this stanza?

Which characteristics of God and His Word are in this stanza?

ZAYIN NOTES

What are the benefits of God's Word in this stanza?

How does the unfolding of this stanza give light (understanding) and life (sustain you)?

74

Light & Life

ZAYIN NOTES

Write a prayer: ....

....

....

....

....

....

....

....

....

....

....

....

....

....

....

....

....

....

....

....

....

....

....

....

Because God's Word is: ....

I can: ....

ZAYIN NOTES

Light & Life

WEEK 3 TEACHING NOTES

WEEK 3 TEACHING NOTES

Light & Life

WEEK 3 GROUP NOTES

READ: ISAIAH 55:10–11

What truths does this passage reveal about God's Word?

Light & Life

WEEK 4

Heth

VERSES 57–64

Light & Life

PSALM 119:57-64

Write the stanza:

Light & Life

HETH NOTES

What are the synonyms for the Word used in this stanza?

Which characteristics of God and His Word are in this stanza?

HETH NOTES

What are the benefits of God's Word in this stanza?

How does the unfolding of this stanza give light (understanding) and life (sustain you)?

HETH NOTES

Write a prayer: ....

....

....

....

....

....

....

....

....

....

....

....

....

....

....

....

....

....

....

....

....

Because God's Word is: ....

I can: ....

HETH NOTES

Teth

VERSES 65-72

PSALM 119:65–72

Write the stanza:

Light & Life

TETH NOTES

What are the synonyms for the Word used in this stanza?

Which characteristics of God and His Word are in this stanza?

What are the benefits of God's Word in this stanza?

How does the unfolding of this stanza give light (understanding) and life (sustain you)?

Light & Life

TETH NOTES

Write a prayer: ....

....

....

....

....

....

....

....

....

....

....

....

....

....

....

....

....

....

....

....

....

....

Because God's Word is: ....

    I can: ....

Light & Life

TETH NOTES

94

Yodh

VERSES 73–80

Light & Life

PSALM 119:73-80

Write the stanza:

YODH NOTES

What are the synonyms for the Word used in this stanza?

Which characteristics of God and His Word are in this stanza?

97

What are the benefits of God's Word in this stanza?

How does the unfolding of this stanza give light (understanding) and life (sustain you)?

YODH NOTES

Write a prayer:

Because God's Word is:

I can:

YODH NOTES

Light & Life

WEEK 4 TEACHING NOTES

Light & Life

WEEK 4 TEACHING NOTES

Light & Life

WEEK 4 GROUP NOTES

READ: JOHN 17:17

What truths does this passage reveal about God's Word?

Light & Life

WEEK 5

Kaph

VERSES 81–88

Light & Life

KAPH NOTES

PSALM 119:81-88

Write the stanza:

Light & Life

What are the synonyms for the Word used in this stanza?

Which characteristics of God and His Word are in this stanza?

Light & Life

What are the benefits of God's Word in this stanza?

How does the unfolding of this stanza give light (understanding) and life (sustain you)?

KAPH NOTES

Write a prayer:

Because God's Word is:

I can:

KAPH NOTES

Lamedh

VERSES 89–96

PSALM 119:89-96

Write the stanza:

Light & Life

What are the synonyms for the Word used in this stanza?

Which characteristics of God and His Word are in this stanza?

Light & Life

LAMEDH NOTES

What are the benefits of God's Word in this stanza?

How does the unfolding of this stanza give light (understanding) and life (sustain you)?

Light & Life

LAMEDH NOTES

Write a prayer: ....

....

....

....

....

....

....

....

....

....

....

....

....

....

....

....

....

....

....

....

....

Because God's Word is: ....

I can: ....

Light & Life

LAMEDH NOTES

Mem

VERSES 97-104

MEM NOTES

PSALM 119:97–104

Write the stanza:

What are the synonyms for the Word used in this stanza?

Which characteristics of God and His Word are in this stanza?

Light & Life

MEM NOTES

What are the benefits of God's Word in this stanza?

How does the unfolding of this stanza give light (understanding) and life (sustain you)?

122

Light & Life

MEM NOTES

Write a prayer:

Because God's Word is:

    I can:

123

MEM NOTES

Light & Life

WEEK 5 TEACHING NOTES

WEEK 5 TEACHING NOTES

Light & Life

WEEK 5 GROUP NOTES

Light & Life

GO DEEPER

READ: JOHN 1:1-14

What truths does this passage reveal about God's Word?

128

Light & Life

WEEK 6

Nun

VERSES 105-112

NUN NOTES

PSALM 119:105-112

Write the stanza:

NUN NOTES

What are the synonyms for the Word used in this stanza?

Which characteristics of God and His Word are in this stanza?

NUN NOTES

What are the benefits of God's Word in this stanza?

How does the unfolding of this stanza give light (understanding) and life (sustain you)?

134

NUN NOTES

Write a prayer: ....

....

....

....

....

....

....

....

....

....

....

....

....

....

....

....

....

....

....

....

....

....

....

Because God's Word is: ....

    I can: ....

Light & Life

NUN NOTES

Samekh

VERSES 113-120

PSALM 119:113-120

Write the stanza:

Light & Life

SAMEKH NOTES

What are the synonyms for the Word used in this stanza?

Which characteristics of God and His Word are in this stanza?

Light & Life

SAMEKH NOTES

What are the benefits of God's Word in this stanza?

How does the unfolding of this stanza give light (understanding) and life (sustain you)?

Light & Life

SAMEKH NOTES

Write a prayer:

Because God's Word is:

I can:

SAMEKH NOTES

Ayin

VERSES 121–128

Light & Life

AYIN NOTES

PSALM 119:121–128

Write the stanza:

Light & Life

AYIN NOTES

What are the synonyms for the Word used in this stanza?

Which characteristics of God and His Word are in this stanza?

What are the benefits of God's Word in this stanza?

How does the unfolding of this stanza give light (understanding) and life (sustain you)?

AYIN NOTES

Write a prayer: ....

Because God's Word is: ....

    I can: ....

147

AYIN NOTES

Light & Life

WEEK 6 TEACHING NOTES

WEEK 6 TEACHING NOTES

Light & Life

WEEK 6 GROUP NOTES

READ: PSALM 1

What truths does this passage reveal about God's Word?

Light & Life

WEEK 7

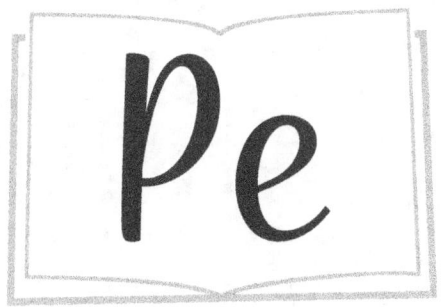

Pe

VERSES 129-136

PE NOTES

PSALM 119:129–136

Write the stanza:

What are the synonyms for the Word used in this stanza?

Which characteristics of God and His Word are in this stanza?

What are the benefits of God's Word in this stanza?

How does the unfolding of this stanza give light (understanding) and life (sustain you)?

Write a prayer: ....

....

....

....

....

....

....

....

....

....

....

....

....

....

....

....

....

....

....

....

....

Because God's Word is: ....

    I can: ....

PE NOTES

Tsadhe

VERSES 137–144

PSALM 119:137–144

Write the stanza:

Light & Life

TSADHE NOTES

What are the synonyms for the Word used in this stanza?

Which characteristics of God and His Word are in this stanza?

163

Light & Life

TSADHE NOTES

What are the benefits of God's Word in this stanza?

How does the unfolding of this stanza give light (understanding) and life (sustain you)?

164

Light & Life

TSADHE NOTES

Write a prayer: ....

....

....

....

....

....

....

....

....

....

....

....

....

....

....

....

....

....

....

....

....

Because God's Word is: ....

I can: ....

Light & Life

TSADHE NOTES

Qoph

VERSES 145–152

Light & Life

QOPH NOTES

PSALM 119:145–152

Write the stanza:

QOPH NOTES

What are the synonyms for the Word used in this stanza?

Which characteristics of God and His Word are in this stanza?

Light & Life

QOPH NOTES

What are the benefits of God's Word in this stanza?

How does the unfolding of this stanza give light (understanding) and life (sustain you)?

170

QOPH NOTES

Write a prayer:

Because God's Word is:

I can:

Light & Life

QOPH NOTES

Light & Life

WEEK 7 TEACHING NOTES

Light & Life

WEEK 7 TEACHING NOTES

Light & Life

WEEK 7 GROUP NOTES

GO DEEPER

READ: 2 TIMOTHY 2:15

What truths does this passage reveal about God's Word?

Light & Life

WEEK 8

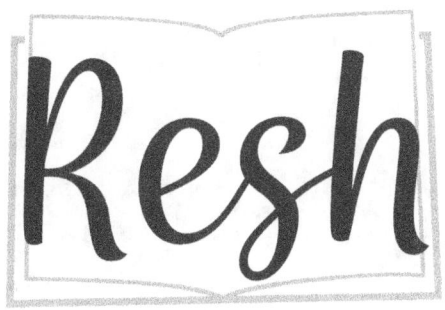

Resh

VERSES 153-160

RESH NOTES

PSALM 119:153-160

Write the stanza:

What are the synonyms for the Word used in this stanza?

Which characteristics of God and His Word are in this stanza?

What are the benefits of God's Word in this stanza?

How does the unfolding of this stanza give light (understanding) and life (sustain you)?

Light & Life

RESH NOTES

Write a prayer: ....

....

....

....

....

....

....

....

....

....

....

....

....

....

....

....

....

....

....

....

....

....

....

Because God's Word is: ....

I can: ....

FRESH NOTES

Sin & Shin

VERSES 161–168

Light & Life

SIN & SHIN NOTES

PSALM 119:161–168

Write the stanza:

Light & Life

SIN & SHIN NOTES

What are the synonyms for the Word used in this stanza?

Which characteristics of God and His Word are in this stanza?

Light & Life

SIN & SHIN NOTES

What are the benefits of God's Word in this stanza?

How does the unfolding of this stanza give light (understanding) and life (sustain you)?

188

SIN & SHIN NOTES

Write a prayer:

Because God's Word is:

    I can:

SIN & SHIN NOTES

190

Taw

VERSES 169-176

TAW NOTES

PSALM 119:169–176

Write the stanza:

192

Light & Life

TAW NOTES

What are the synonyms for the Word used in this stanza?

Which characteristics of God and His Word are in this stanza?

What are the benefits of God's Word in this stanza?

How does the unfolding of this stanza give light (understanding) and life (sustain you)?

Light & Life

TAW NOTES

Write a prayer: ....

....

....

....

....

....

....

....

....

....

....

....

....

....

....

....

....

....

....

....

....

....

Because God's Word is: ....

    I can: ....

TAW NOTES

196

Light & Life

WEEK 8 TEACHING NOTES

Light & Life

WEEK 8 TEACHING NOTES

Light & Life

WEEK 8 GROUP NOTES

199

WEEK 8 GROUP NOTES

Light & Life

ADDITIONAL NOTES

ADDITIONAL NOTES

CHARACTERISTICS OF THE WORD

OTHER SCRIPTURES ABOUT THE WORD

Light & Life

ADDITIONAL NOTES

BENEFITS OF THE WORD

Light & Life

ADDITIONAL NOTES

Light & Life

ADDITIONAL NOTES

Light & Life

ADDITIONAL NOTES

206

four simple questions

Good Bible study is rooted in asking the right questions of Scripture. Our first inclination in Bible study is often to ask, "What does this mean to me?" We want to cut right to the ending. Instead, learning to first understand the context, summary, and character of God in the passage will help us better discern the meaning and our response. I have adopted what I call *Four Simple Questions* as the foundation of my time in the Word. Yes, this takes a little more time and effort, but the practice of persevering through the Word is a valuable one. These four simple questions, as well as other helpful tips and resources for inductive study, are further explained in my book, *Feasting on Truth: Savor the Life-giving Word of God.*

START WITH CONTEXT

It's important to remember that while the Bible was written for us and is applicable to our lives today (Hebrews 4:12), we are not the original audience. It is a book not written in modern America, but in the ancient Middle East. If we do not first answer some key questions to understand the context, we cannot properly understand the passage and its intent. Most of these answers can be found in a good study Bible. Because we are studying a chapter, not a book, of the Bible, it may be harder to find some of these answers. Don't stress! You can find information on trusted Bible study websites as well.

FOUR SIMPLE QUESTIONS

I realized that one of my downfalls when attempting to read and study the Bible for myself was not knowing which questions to ask. Many of the methods I tried were either too open or too rigid. Asking four simple questions provided the right balance of structure and flexibility I needed. I want to release you from thinking this has to look a certain way—it doesn't. Basically: Are you showing up? Are you changing? Are you connected? Does that make you want to keep

207

showing up? If you answer yes to all of these, then you're on the right track! Here is a brief overview of each question:

1. **What does this say?**
Before we can interpret Scripture, we need to know what's going on in the passage. Some methods would call this *observation* or the *aim of the passage.*

   - Write a 1–2 sentence summary of what the passage is about—no interpretation, just the facts.

   - Answer the questions: Who? What? Where? When?

   - Are there any repeated words or phrases?

   - Are there any transitional words (therefore, so, but, and, etc.)? Remember, every word is there for a reason.

2. **What does this say about God?**
This to me has been the most transformative question to ask during Bible study. This book is not about us; it's about God. His character and name are written on every page. Before we can understand our response, we must know who He is.

   - What names of God are used? (His names speak to His character.)

   - What characteristics of God are in this passage?

   - I include Jesus in this as well: What does this passage tell us about Jesus?

   - You can find lists of the names and characteristics of God on pages 12–13.

   - Each week, complete the sentence "Because God is _____, I can _____."

3. **What does this mean?**
PRAY. PRAY. PRAY. Ask the Holy Spirit to guide you in this. Using context, the summary, and other observations you have made, begin to be a detective. Remember the lens through which you are looking. Yes, this takes work, but it's worth doing!

   - Read the passage in multiple translations. What differences do you see?

   - Look up words in the English dictionary.

   - What other passages in Scripture are related to this one? (These are called cross-references.)

   - Read a trusted commentary or study Bible.

   - Research the original language (the Old Testament was originally written in Hebrew and the New Testament in Greek).

   - Go to FeastingOnTruth.com/Resources for recommended resources, Bibles, and commentaries.

4. **How should I respond?**
Our Bible study should change us. John 17:17 says, "Sanctify them in the truth; your word is truth." *Sanctify* is a big churchy word that means "to purify or to make holy." It's the act of separating ourselves from the actions of our flesh and dedicating more of our lives and actions to God. God's Word has a purpose in our lives (Isaiah 55:10–11), and we shouldn't stop at knowing its meaning. Instead, we should respond:

208

- Is there an action I need to take?

- A conversation I need to have?

- A moment of worship?

- Something I should let go?

- Write out a prayer.

However you feel led to respond, write it down and enlist someone to hold you accountable.

OTHER HELPFUL TIPS

Listen to the Passage

Use a Bible app to listen to the passages each week. We often feel like this is a cop-out, but for thousands of years, the Word of God was passed down orally from generation to generation. It's a book meant to be read out loud, and when you listen to it, you'll be amazed at how much you pick up on that you didn't notice when reading it.

Use Different Colored Pens

I've found using different colored pens when writing my study notes helps me remember where the note came from. For instance, I use different colors for rewriting the Scripture verses, my thoughts, certain study Bibles, cross-references or different translations, commentary quotes, and Greek or Hebrew word definitions. I don't really have a color system, so the colors change from time to time. That's okay too!

Start with a Clean Copy of God's Word

A study Bible adds additional commentary. Using a Bible that doesn't have any additional commentary removes the temptation to peek at notes before fully understanding the passage on your own. If you do not have a non-study Bible, don't fret! You can print out chapters on several Bible websites including www.BibleGateway.com. I use an ESV journaling Bible for my initial study (which has very few footnotes), then move to other versions and other study Bibles as I go through my study week. Speaking of translations . . .

A Note About Translations

There are a myriad of translations out there, so how do you know which to pick? First, it's important to know where translations come from. The Old Testament was originally written in Hebrew, while the New Testament was written in Greek (though a few portions were written in Aramaic).

Over the years, translators have used original copies written in these languages to interpret Scripture into English (and other languages as well). Translations fall on a spectrum between two ends: word-for-word (translations that use the closest English word to the original word) and thought-for-thought (translations that rephrase the words into more modern, understandable English). Technically, all of them are a mix of the two, but some lean more toward one end or the other.

Some examples of translations that lean toward word-for-word include: English Standard Version (ESV—my top choice), New American Standard Bible (NAS or NASB), and King James Version (KJV). These are the closest to the original language, but we can sometimes miss the cultural context.

An example of thought-for-thought is the New Living Translation (NLT).

There are also versions that are more toward the middle of the spectrum, such as the Christian Standard Bible (CSB) and the New International Version (NIV).

The last kind of translation is not necessarily a translation at all, but rather a paraphrase. Paraphrase Bibles, like *The Message*, should be treated more like commentary because, while they can bring insight into the meaning of the passage, they are not Scripture themselves. I rarely use this type. If you do use a paraphrase, wait until you've completed questions 1–3 and are consulting other commentaries for additional insights.

Let's Feast!

See? Simple. Yes, it takes practice, but honestly, it doesn't take as long as you'd think. You just have to be willing to spend time with Jesus. In Acts 4, Peter and John are on trial before the religious leaders (the smartest of the smart when it came to the Law), and in verse 13 it says, "Now when they saw the boldness of Peter and John, and perceived that they were uneducated, common men, they were astonished. And they recognized that they had been with Jesus." Uneducated. Common. Peter and John hadn't been to seminary, but they had been *with* Jesus.

What I've found is that there is not one method that will make all of this work for you. The power is not in the method. The power is in the Word of God. The power is in spending time with Jesus in the Word with the Holy Spirit as your guide.

When you see your life change and you find community around the Word, you will find yourself returning to Scripture, growing more confident as you study, and discovering the joy and excitement of Feasting on Truth.

Visit FeastingOnTruth.com/HowTo for more information
and in-depth teachings on these questions.

feasting at the table

I may be from Florida, but my family has Southern roots. That means macaroni-and-cheese is considered a vegetable (okay—not really, but why is it an option on vegetable plates at restaurants??). A good macaroni-and-cheese recipe is a staple for any southern cook, and my mom always made the best homemade macaroni-and-cheese. It was baked and had a yummy crust of melted cheese on top. As I began making my own, I didn't always have time (or patience) to bake it, and I grew to love the creaminess of stove-top mac-n-cheese (abbreviated because it's a shortcut recipe). Plus, it's almost as easy as a box, and it's ready in under 30 minutes. Delicious and quick! That's a win for any busy cook.

Quality matters when it comes to cooking. Using higher quality ingredients will yield a more flavorful dish. Don't buy shredded cheese. I know it's an extra step to shred your own, but the additives used to keep the shredded cheese from sticking will keep your sauce from being super creamy. The sour cream adds an extra layer of creaminess with a hint of tang, and the mustard is the secret to this recipe. My mom used mustard powder, but one day I was out of it (and honestly, this was the only recipe I ever used it in). I tried good ol' yellow mustard, and it worked! And that's something I always have on hand.

This recipe can stand on its own as a main dish for a meatless meal, or you can serve it alongside grilled chicken and roasted broccoli for a well-rounded dinner. It's also a great option for a potluck! Oh, and let me reassure you: I have three kids—box macaroni-and-cheese makes an appearance every now and then in our house too. Enjoy!

ERIN'S MAC-N-CHEESE

Time: 25–30 minutes
Yield: 6–8 servings

INGREDIENTS

16 ounce box of shaped pasta (pick your favorite: elbows, pipe rigate, bowtie, penne, etc.)
8 ounce block of sharp cheddar, shredded (white or yellow is fine, but I prefer white cheddar)

3 tablespoons butter
3 tablespoons all-purpose flour
1½ cups milk

½ teaspoon yellow mustard
¼ cup sour cream

2–3 tablespoons kosher salt

INSTRUCTIONS

1. In a large pot of boiling, salted water (2–3 tablespoons kosher salt) add the pasta and cook one minute short of the package instructions. Drain and set aside (do not rinse).

2. In the same pot, over medium-low heat, melt the butter. Add the flour and whisk briskly for about one minute (this cooks off the flour taste and makes a roux—a thickener for the cheese sauce). Add one cup of the milk and whisk quickly until smooth. As the sauce begins to thicken, add the remaining half cup of milk.

3. Stir in the mustard and sour cream. Stir until incorporated.

4. Add cheese and stir until melted.

5. Stir in the pasta and serve hot!

about Erin

ERIN H. WARREN is passionate about equipping and encouraging women to discover God's truths for themselves. She is the author of *Feasting on Truth: Savor the Life-giving Word of God*, leads and teaches Bible study through her ministry Feasting on Truth, and has published several Bible studies. She and her husband, Kris, have three littles (who aren't so little anymore), and they live in Central Florida. She loves a house full of people and a table full of food and hopes tacos never go out of style. You can find more information about Feasting on Truth on her website: FeastingOnTruth.com. You can also connect with her on Instagram: @erinhwarren and @feastingontruth and YouTube: www.youtube.com/c/erinhwarren.

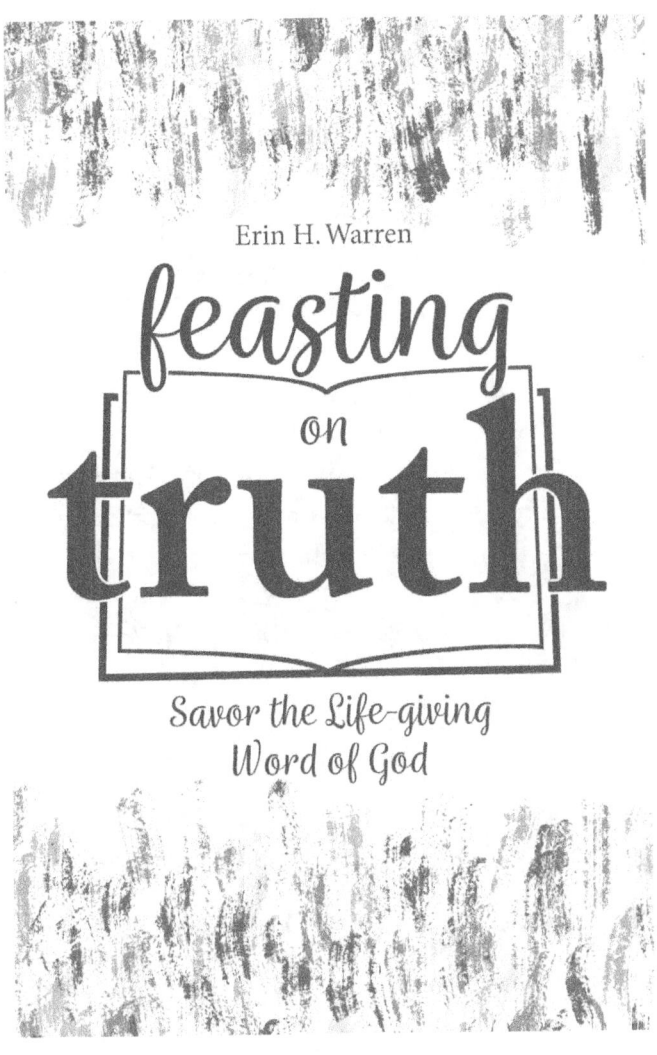

Erin H. Warren

feasting on truth

Savor the Life-giving
Word of God

FEASTING ON TRUTH
SAVOR THE LIFE-GIVING WORD OF GOD

The Word of God is our very life, but Erin Warren felt anything but alive. Her husband was sick. Her world was falling apart, and she had questions. Feel-good faith was not enough; she needed deep, sustaining truths.

Through her own wrestling, Erin Warren addresses the obstacles that held her back when it came to Bible study and how she discovered to savor the life-giving Word of God.

The word *feast* is rooted in abundance. That is what awaits us in the pages of Scripture: a table laid out before us, not only for our essential nourishment, but for our enjoyment.

FeastingOnTruth.com/Books

STORIES FROM THE WILDERNESS

A STUDY OF THE ISRAELITES' JOURNEY FROM EGYPT TO THE PROMISED LAND

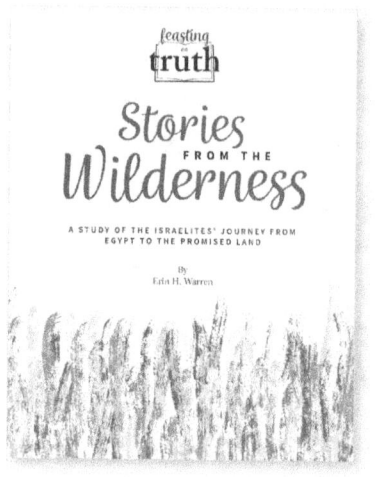

The wilderness. It is a place that feels hard, empty, lifeless, and pathless, and it often leaves us with questions about who God is. But where we see a place that is worthless, confusing, and chaotic, God sees a place to display His power. Time and time again throughout Scripture, God takes the worthless, seemingly wasteful, confusing, chaotic, and empty places and uses them as a backdrop to prove His character, draw us in, and display His glory.

FeastingOnTruth.com/Wilderness

TO DWELL IN OUR MIDST

A STUDY OF THE TABERNACLE AND HOW IT POINTS US TO JESUS

Why study this ancient tent? What does knowing about the Tabernacle have to do with our faith on this side of the cross? Everything. This tent is not merely ritual or history or good information—it's essential to understanding our salvation. Our detailed and deliberate God gave us the Tabernacle because one day, He would give us Jesus. It's an invitation into a relationship with our Holy God. Discover God's plan to dwell in our midst through Jesus Christ.

FeastingOnTruth.com/Dwell